HOME DECOR CHEAT SHEETS

NEED-TO-KNOW STUFF FOR STYLISH LIVING

JESSICA PROBUS

Illustrated by Alice Mongkongllite

Ulysses Press

Published in the US by:
ULYSSES PRESS
PO Box 3440
Berkeley, CA 94703
www.ulyssespress.com

ISBN: 978-1-61243-554-1
Library of Congresss Conrol Number: 2015952123

Printed in Korea by WE SP through Four Colour Print Group

10 9 8 7 6 5 4 3 2 1

Acquisitions editor: Casie Vogel
Managing editor: Claire Chun
Copy editor: Renee Rutledge
Cover design: Alice Mongkongllite
Interior design: Jake Flaherty

Distributed by Publishers Group West

*To my mom and dad, who knew how to make every space into a home, and to
Caroline, who gave my wild heart a place to nest.*
—JP

To my mom, Ray, Michael, and Loki.
—AM

Contents

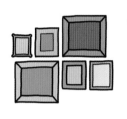

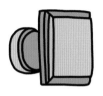

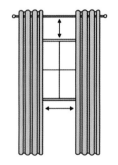

INTRODUCTION

The path to one's dream home is often littered with obstacles and complications—money, location, timing, furnishings, and everything in between. This book is meant to simplify all of that. These cheat sheets are here to provide uncomplicated ways to make anywhere you reside a more functional, warm, and open space where the furnishings and decor aren't the main attraction, but instead are the seamless backdrop for the kind of life you want to live there.

Whether you're still looking for your first apartment or moving into your seventeenth home, the tips in this book will help you make small adjustments that can have a big impact, from raising the curtains to make a ceiling look higher to moving a table to allow for better walking space. And whether you have your heart set on an ikat cabriole or you can't tell the difference between a chaise lounge and a chesterfield, these visual guides will make each of these tips easy to understand.

Just like the completion of any home, the cheat sheets in this book are meant to be used as a process not to be tackled in one day or even one year, but consulted as needed over time to make the kind of slow, purposeful improvements that turn a few walls and some well-hung curtains into an actual home. And while many of these "rules" are designed to make your space more comfortable and functional, the most important reason to learn any rules is to know when and how to break them.

How to Use This Book

Furniture styles can be divided into three main categories: modern, transitional, and classic. While most homes have an eclectic mix of all these styles, if you're not sure what you like, here's a basic explanation of how these terms are used in this book:

Modern refers to a more streamlined look with clean lines and minimalist shapes. Modern furniture is often done in lighter woods, or alternative materials like metallics or molded plastics.

Transitional style furniture is often a mix of wood and upholstery, with soft lines and simple silhouettes that can work in lots of different homes. Transitional furniture is more relaxed, with more cushioning and less defined features than modern or classic styles.

Classic refers to an older and more traditional look of furniture, like reproduction antiques. Classic furniture is often made with dark woods, curved lines, and heavy fabrics like brocades and velvets, and is usually less comfortable than transitional or modern styles.

Some of these cheat sheets can be used simply to improve your design vocabulary, which will give you a leg up when talking to salespeople or searching online for your ideal look; searching for a "tight back Lawson" will get you much better results than just searching "sofa." For those who already have a good idea of their home style, other sections will give you some tricks to take each room's design to the next level and add the finishing touches to any space that still needs a little work. Finally, if you get through this book and make all the improvements you need, the Resource Guide at the end of the book will give you tons more places to continue your home design education.

LIVING ROOM

Sofa Styles

Choosing a sofa is a big decision, not only because of the cost, but also because they set the tone for the style of the room. While all furniture designers and manufacturers have their own unique names for their sofa models, these are 10 of the most common silhouettes and names for sofa styles, ranging from a more traditional Old World look to a sleek, modern shape.

MODERN

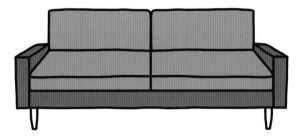

Mid-Century

Daybed

Chaise

TRANSITIONAL

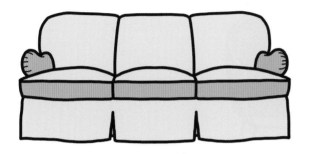

English Roll Arm

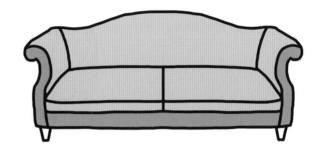

Camelback

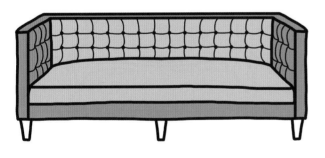

Tuxedo

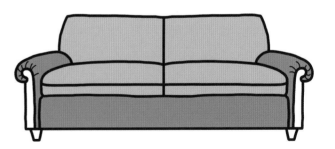

Lawson

CLASSIC

Cabriole

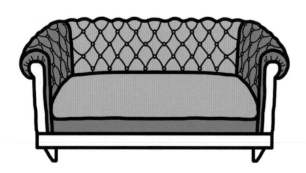

Chesterfield

Settee

Sofa Glossary

Bench Seat: A single cushion that goes the entire length of the sofa.

Camelback: A common type sofa which has a back that's highest in the middle, shaped like a camel's hump.

Deck: The bottom structure of the sofa where the seat cushions rest. In loose-cushion models, the deck is usually upholstered in a neutral-colored fabric instead of the upholstery material.

Left-Arm or Right-Arm: Used to describe which side a chaise is located on a sectional when you are facing the sofa.

Loose Cushion: A sofa which has cushions that are not attached to the sofa base. These tend to be very comfortable and easier to clean. Some models can have a pillow back with tight seat cushions, some have a tight back with loose seat cushions.

Pillow Back: Another term for loose-cushion models where the cushions are not attached to the deck.

Rolled Arm: A sofa style with arms that curve outward, usually cushioned. This is a classic and traditional sofa style.

Sectional: A sofa that comes in multiple parts that can often be rearranged to make a new shape. The most common is the L-shaped sectional.

Skirt: A section of fabric that extends from the deck of the sofa to the floor, usually covering the legs.

Sleeper: Any sofa that can be adjusted to become a bed, whether it's a pull-out model or a futon style that leans back.

Square Arm: A sofa style with arms that are boxy and usually cushioned. These models are more streamlined and modern.

Tight Back: A sofa with no removable cushions. This minimalist look tends to be less comfortable than loose-cushion models. Instead of a filled cushion, these usually have a spring base.

Tufted: An upholstery style that uses knots or buttons to secure sections of the fabric to the base, resulting in "tufts" of fabric. Tufted sofas have a classic and expensive look but are often less comfortable than other models.

Welt: A decorative cord used as an accent along the lines of an upholstered piece, sometimes used in a contrasting color from the upholstery.

Upholstered Chair Styles

Upholstered accent chairs are a great way to add extra seating to a space and mix different design styles in one room. A bigger investment, armchairs are more comfortable than occasional chairs, which are smaller and more portable, meeting whatever seating needs arise on any occasion.

PRO TIP: If your sofa and chairs are dramatically different in style, use throw pillows in matching colors or coordinating patterns to tie the space together.

Tub

Wingback

Modern Wingback

Bergère

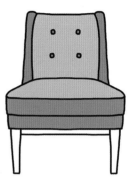

Slipper

Lawson

Club

Occasional

Coffee Table Styles

Coffee tables can make a seating area feel complete and functional. The ideal style and size depends on the size and style of your sofa and other seating in the room. Rectangular tables are the most common and work well with long sofas. Square or round tables are ideal for smaller seating arrangements.

Cottage

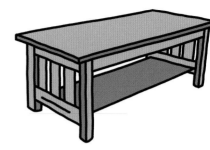

Shaker

Mid-Century

Parsons

Modern

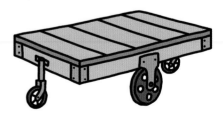

Industrial

Coffee Table Height & Width

The best size for your coffee table depends on the size of your sofa. For optimal balance and function, the coffee table should be around two thirds the width of the sofa, and the height should be 2 to 4 inches below the height of the sofa seat. To give ample room for moving around, make sure there are around 18 inches of space between the sofa and the table.

2–4"

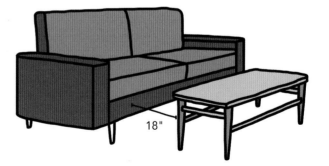

18"

Side Table Styles

To figure out if or where you need a side table, think of it this way: there should be somewhere for someone in every seating position in the room to easily place a drink. In addition to having this functional use, side tables are a great place to put extra lighting or to introduce a different color or texture into a room.

French

Art Deco

Mid-Century

Regency

Tulip

Modern

Industrial

Side Table Height

The ideal height of a side table depends on the height of the arm of the furniture that's next to it: each table should be within 2 inches of the height of the sofa or chair arm. For armless furniture, the table should be within 2 inches of the height of the seat.

2"

6"

2"

DINING ROOM

Dining Table Styles

While the style of your dining table is important, the most crucial thing to consider is the size. To allow for chairs to comfortably move in and out, you need at least 42 to 48 inches between the edge of your table and the walls or nearest piece of furniture. Pedestal tables can usually fit more people than trestle or farmhouse-style tables, because there is more leg room underneath.

MODERN

Pedestal

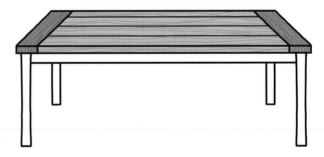

Farmhouse

TRANSITIONAL

CLASSIC

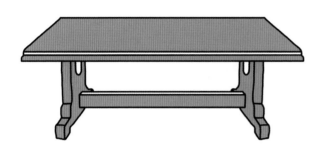

Trestle

Pedestal

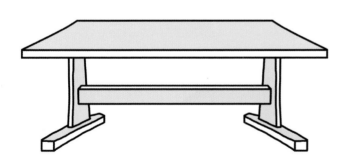

Trestle

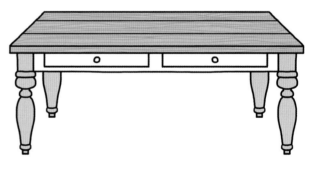

Farmhouse

Dining Table Size: Round

Round dining tables are great for smaller square spaces and can usually fit more people because there are no corners. They make for a cozier and more intimate eating experience since everyone is the same distance apart. This guideline shows the most comfortable number of chairs to put around each size table. If your chairs are larger or have arms, fewer people will fit.

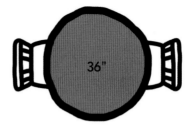

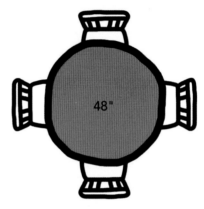

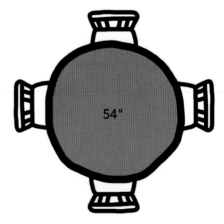

72"

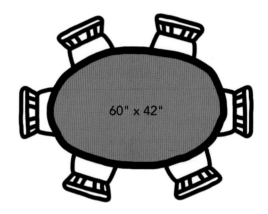

60" x 42"

Dining Table Size: Rectangular

Rectangular tables are ideal for longer rooms, larger groups, or dining spaces with foot traffic going through them. At a rectangular or square table, each person should have 2 feet of eating space, though more chairs can be added for big occasions. Rectangular tables are also great for bench seating, which can be tucked under the table when not in use, making the space less crowded.

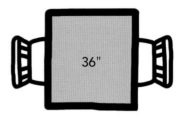

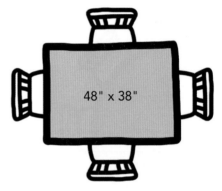

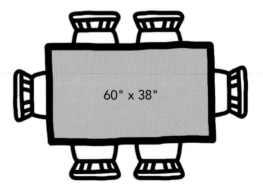

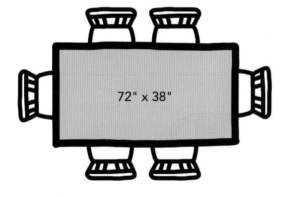

72" x 38"

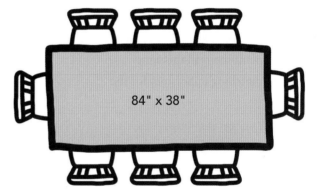

84" x 38"

Dining Chair Styles

The right dining chairs can totally change the look of a table. And if you're feeling brave, mixing and matching a set of dining chairs is a great way to add character to an older dining table without having to buy a whole new set. To make a group of mismatched chairs feel unified, paint them all the same color or use matching upholstery for the cushions.

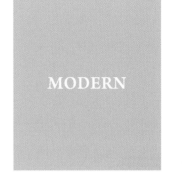

MODERN

Mid-Century Modern

Industrial Cafe

Modern Bentwood

TRANSITIONAL

Windsor

Vintage French

Parsons

CLASSIC

French Bistro

Cross Back

Traditional Bentwood

Kinds of Stools

The kind of stool you choose should depend on the style of your room and how often you plan to use it. Backless stools take up less visual space but are much less comfortable for everyday use. Upholstered or high-back stools are often more expensive and take up more space, but are much more comfortable as actual dining chairs. While classic stools tend to be high-backed and modern or industrial low and un-cushioned, there are a wide range of stool shapes in every style.

Saddle

Industrial

Mid-Century

Retro

Drafting

Fabric

Stool Height

The only difference between bar stools and counter stools is height: bar stools are typically 30 to 32 inches high and counter stools are 24 to 26 inches high. Some stores and manufacturers use these terms interchangeably. No matter what you call it, the key element to choosing your stool height is this: there should be 8 to 10 inches of space in between the bottom of your bar or table and the top of your bar seat.

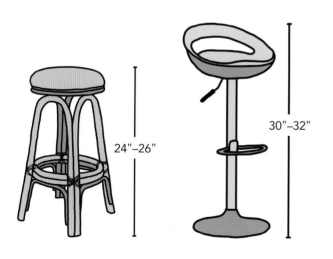

24"–26"

30"–32"

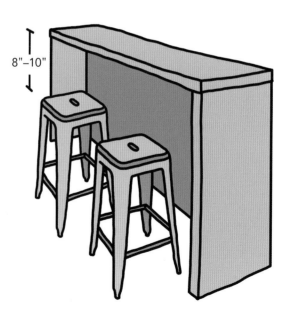

8"–10"

BEDROOM

Bed Styles

Choosing a bed frame is a big decision, similar to choosing a sofa, because of the investment and the way it changes the whole look and feel of a room. Certain bed styles also serve different functions: storage beds, or beds with room for storage underneath, are great for small apartments or spaces. Trundle beds and day beds can function as extra seating or sleeping spaces. Canopy and poster beds make a big visual statement and also divide up a larger space. All of these bed styles are often available in each different bed size.

MODERN

Divan   Platform   Trundle

TRANSITIONAL

Poster

Panel

Upholstered

CLASSIC

Canopy

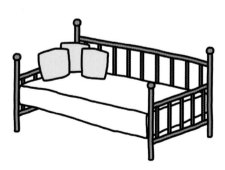

Day

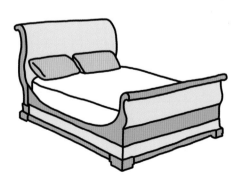

Sleigh

Headboard Styles

Headboards come in many different shapes and sizes, and most of them are given different names from each designer or manufacturer. These terms are a generic way to describe the silhouette that speaks to you, whether you're in the market or want to DIY. A more rounded headboard gives the room a softness, while square or stepped ones can add a masculine vibe.

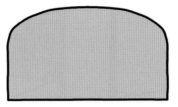

Arch

Basic

Bevel

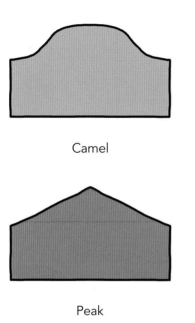

Camel

Peak

Round

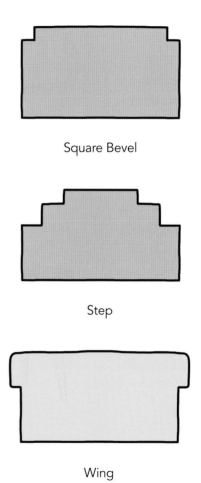

Square Bevel

Step

Wing

Nightstand Styles

Nightstands were originally called "commodes," which comes from the French word for "convenient" because the cabinet concealed a bedside chamber pot. Today, many nightstands still have storage space in drawers or doors. In addition to having storage, nightstands are also a great way to introduce a new color or texture into your bedroom.

Bombe

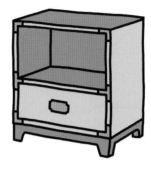

Campaign

Cottage

Mid-century

Shaker

Transitional

Nightstand Height

The ideal height for a nightstand depends on the height of the bed. The standard height range for both nightstands and beds is 24 to 28 inches high, but many older canopy beds or modern platform beds can be significantly different. A good rule of thumb is for the nightstand to be either the same height as the bed or a couple inches higher.

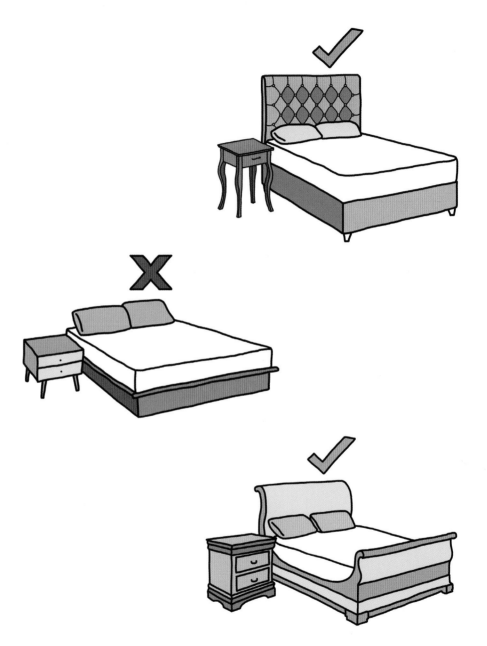

Bed Pillow Arrangements

The number and style of decorative and functional bed pillows you should have depends on two factors: the style of your room and how hard you want it to be to make the bed. These are just a few ways to combine the pillows you actually sleep on with one or more decorative pillows to make your bed feel complete and pulled together. The three kinds of pillows shown here are: simple (functional sleeping pillows), standard (larger square pillows, usually with decorative removable shams), and decorative (smaller square or rectangular pillows, sometimes with removable covers).

TWIN

Simple

Standard

Decorative

FULL & QUEEN

KING

Simple

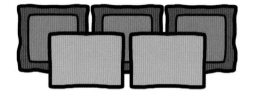

Simple

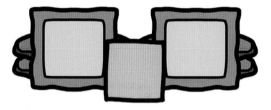

Standard

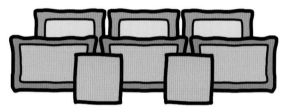

Standard

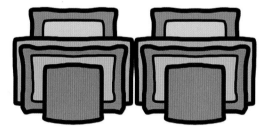

Decorative

Decorative

Bed Sizes

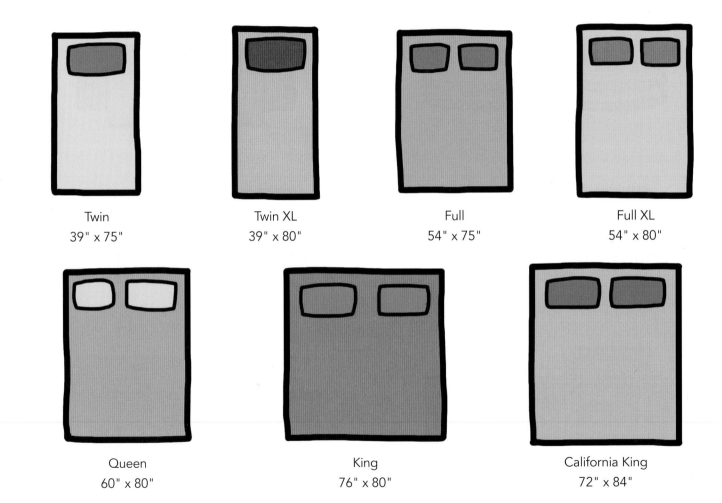

Twin
39" x 75"

Twin XL
39" x 80"

Full
54" x 75"

Full XL
54" x 80"

Queen
60" x 80"

King
76" x 80"

California King
72" x 84"

TILE & RUGS

Tile Patterns

Tile patterns and shapes can change the look and scale of a room completely. Simple layouts, like the stack bond or checkerboard, work in any space and can be used to direct the line of sight toward a focal point in the room. Herringbone or basketweave patterns can be used at an angle to make a small space appear larger. Offset or subway patterns can be used to hide imperfections or uneven room sizes.

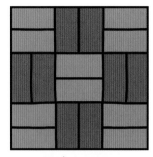

Basketweave

Double Herringbone

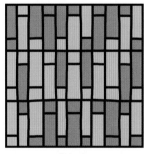

Stitch

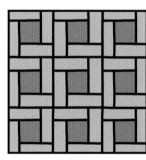

Knit

Herringbone

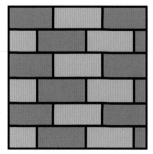

Stagger

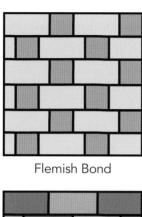

Flemish Bond

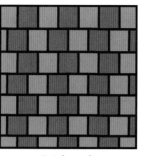

Brickwork

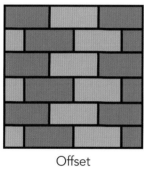

Offset

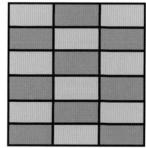

Stack Bond

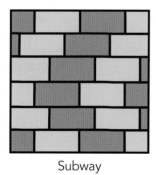

Subway

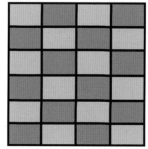

Checkerboard

Living Room Rug Size

When choosing a rug for your living room, consider the size of your seating area. The key elements here are furniture legs. The legs of each seating element (sofa, chairs) should be either all on the rug, all off the rug, or with the front legs of each on the rug and the back legs off. This will make the space feel cohesive and tied together. If you can afford it, the best looking rug is big enough to extend 1 foot past the back legs of each seating element.

GOOD

BETTER

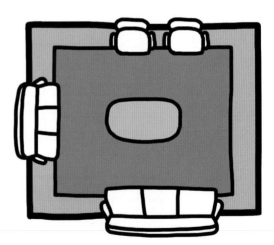

BEST

Dining Room Rug Size

For the dining room, it's key to choose a rug that all the chair and table legs will fit on, even when the chairs are pulled out. A rug that's 3 to 4 feet wider than the table is ideal to make the room feel spacious, but if you need to get a smaller rug, a shape that contrasts with the table shape (i.e., an oval rug with a rectangular table or a rectangular rug with an oval table) will provide enough visual contrast to make it look interesting.

GOOD

BETTER

BEST

Bedroom Rug Size

A good rug can make the bedroom feel infinitely more cozy. The best size and location for the rug is whatever places it directly under your feet when you get out of bed. This can be achieved with a small rug right next to the bed, or a rug large enough for the entire bed and nightstand to rest on it. Large rugs can get very expensive, but the ideal rug size for a bedroom is one that extends at least 1 foot past each nightstand and 2 feet past the end of the bed or any furniture at the bottom of the bed.

GOOD

BETTER

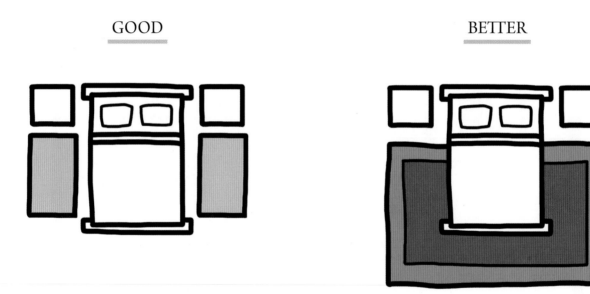

BEST

Rug Glossary

Acrylic: Synthetic fiber used to create a wool-like rug. Cheaper but much less durable than actual wool.

All-Over Design: A rug without a medallion design in the center, but with a patten that covers the entire rug. Usually more contemporary.

Carved Pile: A high pile rug with a pattern or design cut into it. Seen often in Chinese carpet designs.

Cotton: Rugs made with cotton are soft, fairly durable, and usually machine washable.

Dhurrie: A thick, flatweave cotton rug that originated in India. Durable and available in a variety of styles and patterns.

Flatweave: Made with a loom instead of knotting or tufting, these rugs have no pile, and are both durable and reversible.

Hand Knotted: Made with a labor-intensive process that involves individual strands of yarn being knotted around warp threads that run the entire length of the rug. High-quality rugs made this way tend to be more expensive.

Hooked: A tufted rug where the pile is looped instead of cut.

Jute: Natural fiber used to make rugs that are less soft than wool or cotton but very durable.

Kilim: A flatweave rug that is often reversible.

Medallion: The center design element that is often symmetrical in traditional oriental rugs.

Overdyed: Primarily antique wool rugs made through a process of bleaching and then oversaturating the rug with a bright color. Often you can still see hints of the original pattern.

Pile: The term used to refer to the density and length of the rug's fibers. Higher pile rugs are softer, lower pile rugs are more durable.

Silk: Often used in combination with wool to give a rug a particular sheen.

Sisal: Natural fiber similar to jute. Used to make rugs that are less soft than wool or cotton but very durable.

Tufted: Rug-making process that involves pulling loops of yarn through a backing material. Can be made by hand or with a machine.

Viscose: Synthetic material used to make imitation silk rugs. Often sheds and while inexpensive, does not last.

Wool: Versatile material for making higher-end rugs that are both soft and extremely durable. Wool is easily dyed and can be made into many types of rugs, from flatweave to high pile.

WINDOWS & DOORS

Types of Doors

The shape and style of interior doors will depend on the function and size of each room: bi-fold and pocket doors are common on narrow interior spaces like hallways and closets, while flush and French doors are used for passage between larger areas. The shape and style of exterior doors are more decorative or safety-related: doors with more glass (or lite) are usually less safe but also let in more light.

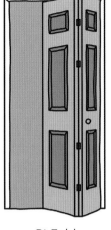

INTERIOR DOORS

Bi-Fold

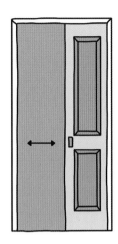

Pocket

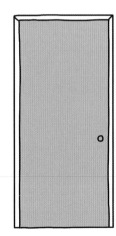

Flush

French

EXTERIOR DOORS

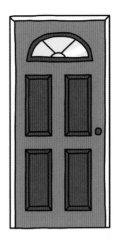

Four Paneled

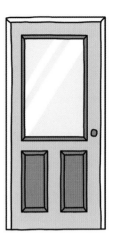

Half Lite

Six Paneled

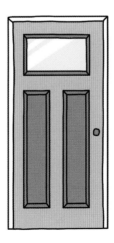

Quarter Lite

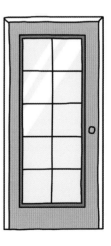

Full Lite

How to Paint a Door

Paneled doors are some of the most commonly used types for interior and exterior purposes because they have great depth and detail.

The vertical panels of a door (1,2,4) are called stiles. The horizontal panels (3) are called rails. The basic rule of thumb for painting like a pro is to paint from the center out.

1. First, paint the door panels and interior molding.

2. Then, paint the middle stile all the way down.

3. Paint all the rails across the door.

4. Finish with the outside border of the entire door.

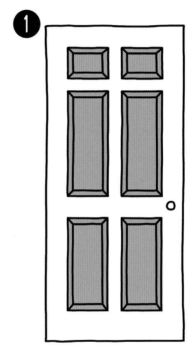

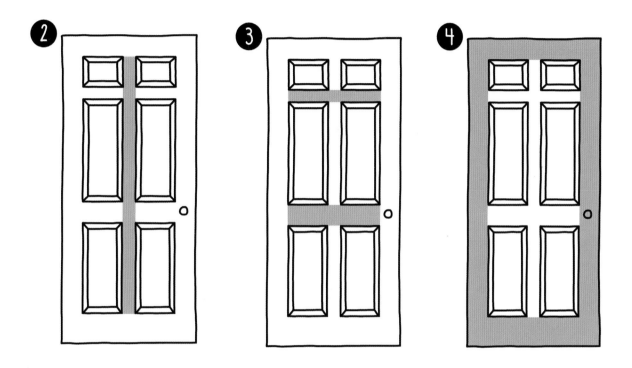

PRO TIP: Paint with the grain, even if it's a fake wood grain. It will keep the brush strokes consistent and natural. Make sure the door is totally clean! Paint magnifies imperfections and will peel faster when applied to a door that has any debris. It's a lot easier to avoid drips when you take the door all the way off its hinges and lay it out flat. It takes a little extra time to do all the work, but it looks much better in the end.

Basic Window Styles

Most homes have multiple kinds of windows throughout depending on the room location and function. Window types are defined by where the hinges are located (if any) and how they open. Single and double hung windows have a more traditional look and are usually cheaper than casement windows that open from the side. Double hung windows provide a natural convection when both the top and bottom sashes are open. Casement windows provide superior ventilation when open and insulation and noise reduction when closed. Picture or stationary windows do not open, so they provide better insulation and natural light than other styles.

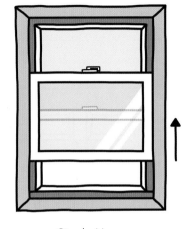

Single Hung

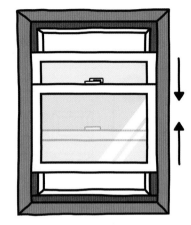

Double Hung

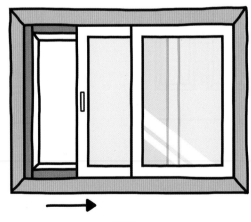

Sliding

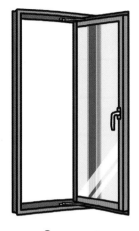

Casement

Awning

French

Picture

Leaded Window Styles

Leadlight or came glass is a simple type of glasswork that involves making small pieces of glass into a larger decorative window. These were common on homes and cottages dating from the early twentieth century, and can still be found in many homes from the era and in thrift stores as standalone decorative pieces.

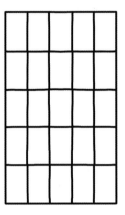

Georgian

Diamond

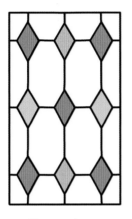

Queen Anne

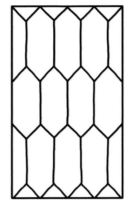

Tudor

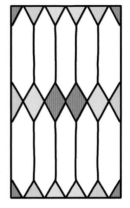

Regent

Boxed Diamond

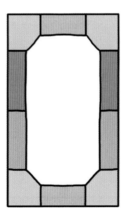

Gothic

Mosaic

Types of Blinds

Blinds are an excellent way to add privacy to a room without the cluttered look that curtains often give. The type you choose is largely a matter of preference, though a thicker vertical blind can make a room feel smaller or more crowded when used on multiple windows.

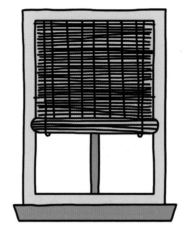

Matchstick

Venetian

Mini Venetian

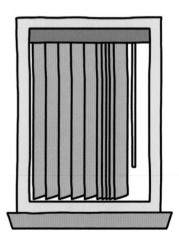

Vertical

Types of Shades

Like blinds, the type of shade you choose is an aesthetic choice more than a functional one. Roller and Roman shades are usually more modern than tie-ups, but a different fabric choice can make any of these types work in multiple styles.

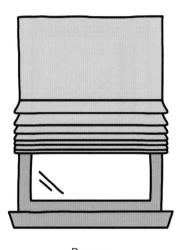

Roman

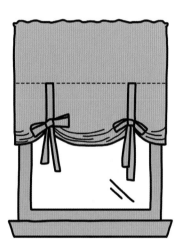

Tie-Up

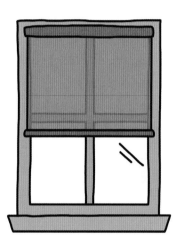

Roller

Mounting Options

The way you mount your blinds will depend on the shape and size of your window and how much darkness you want in the space. While there's no right or wrong way to mount, and there are benefits to both an interior and exterior mount, some windows might only work with one mounting style.

INTERIOR MOUNT

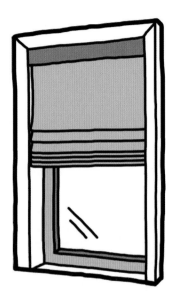

Pros: For windows with decorative trim, mounting your blinds on the interior of the window is a great way to show that off, as long as your windows are deep-set enough to hold them. This can also make the space feel bigger, since the shades won't take up any extra depth.

Cons: This isn't ideal if you want total darkness since there will likely be a gap between the shade and the frame. And for shorter windows, the blinds will obscure some of the view when they're up since they bunch at the top of the frame.

EXTERIOR MOUNT

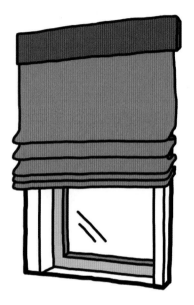

Pros: Mounting your blinds outside and above your window can make the window itself appear bigger, and also allow all the light from the window inside the room. If you don't have decorative window frames, this mounting style can add a little extra style to the space.

Cons: This style takes up more room on your wall and can make the space feel a little smaller, especially if the blinds themselves are dark.

Types of Curtains

Choose your curtain hanging according to your style preference—tab and grommet curtains tend to be a little more modern, while pocket and pleat curtains are more traditional.

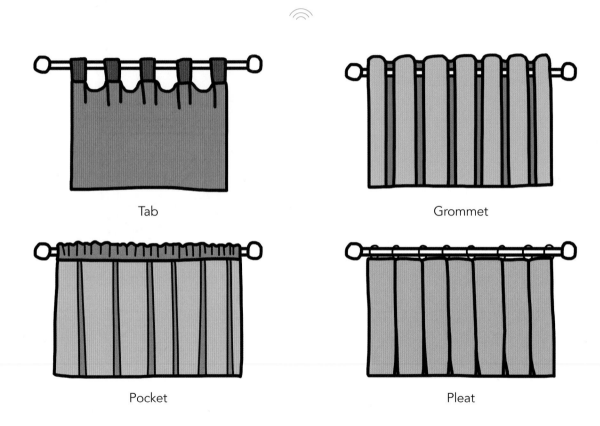

Tab

Grommet

Pocket

Pleat

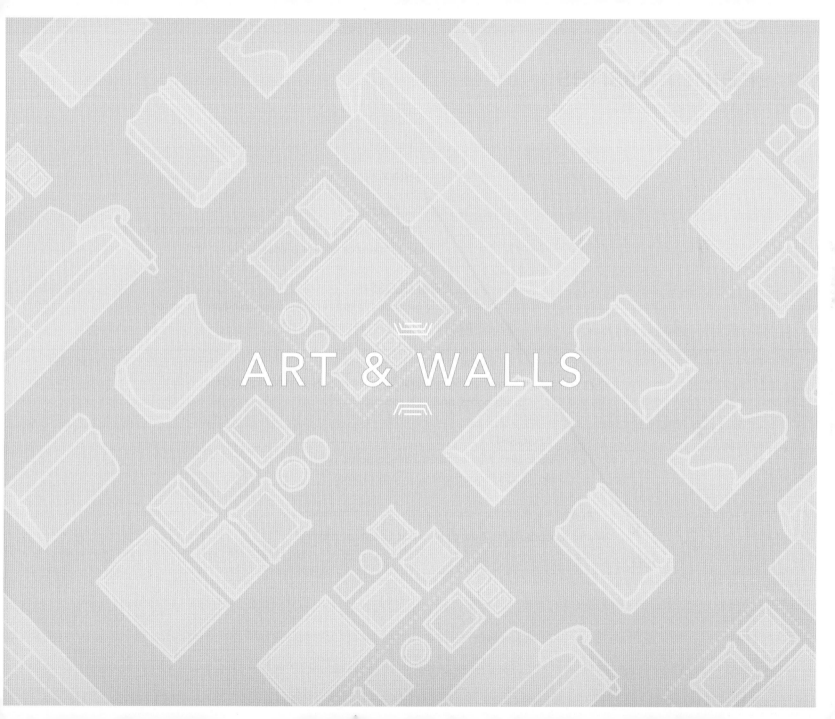

Paint Finishes

SHINY

GLOSS
Mirror-like reflection, shows imperfections easily. Ideal for furniture or accent pieces.

SEMI-GLOSS
Highly reflective, extra durable, easy to clean. Used for trim, molding, and cabinets.

SATIN
Reflects light, durable, wipes clean. Perfect for kitchens, bathrooms, and kids rooms.

EGGSHELL
Matte with a little sheen, reflects some light, hard to clean. Good for bedrooms, livings rooms.

FLAT
Matte, absorbs light, gets dirty easily. Great for ceilings.

DULL

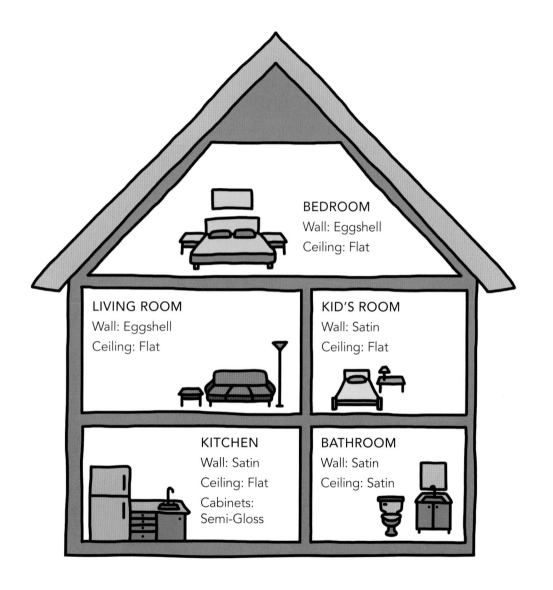

BEDROOM
Wall: Eggshell
Ceiling: Flat

LIVING ROOM
Wall: Eggshell
Ceiling: Flat

KID'S ROOM
Wall: Satin
Ceiling: Flat

KITCHEN
Wall: Satin
Ceiling: Flat
Cabinets:
Semi-Gloss

BATHROOM
Wall: Satin
Ceiling: Satin

Molding Map

1. Crown

2. Cove

3. Chair rail

4. Base cap

5. Baseboard

6. Base shoe

7. Casing

8. Corner guard

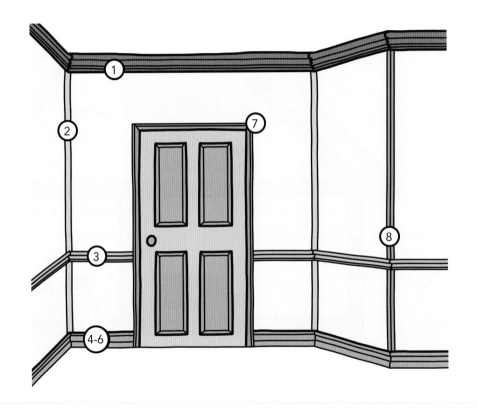

Types of Molding

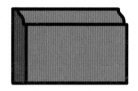

Baseboard

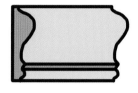

Chair Rail

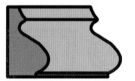

Base Cap

Corner Guard

Base Shoe

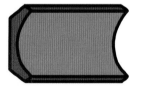

Cove

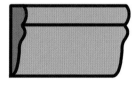

Casing

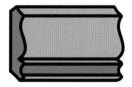

Crown

Gallery Walls 101

The easiest way to start a gallery wall is to place art either surrounding a midline (Diagram A) or inside a contained space (Diagram B).

The width of the gallery wall should be at least two-thirds the size of whatever furniture or focal point it goes above.

For an eclectic look, vary the colors and the size and shape of the frames, and art pieces.

To add cohesion, at least half the pieces or frames should have a similar color or color scheme.

DIAGRAM A

DIAGRAM B

PRO TIP: Try using painter's tape to map out the size of the midline or space as you hang to keep it even.

Gallery Wall Layouts

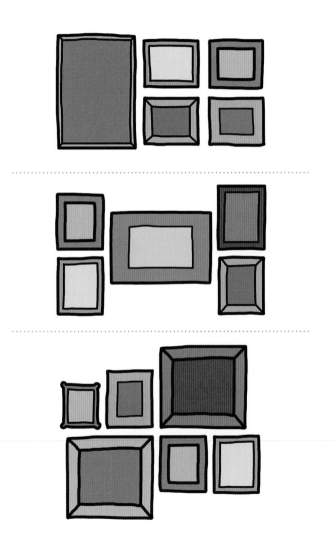

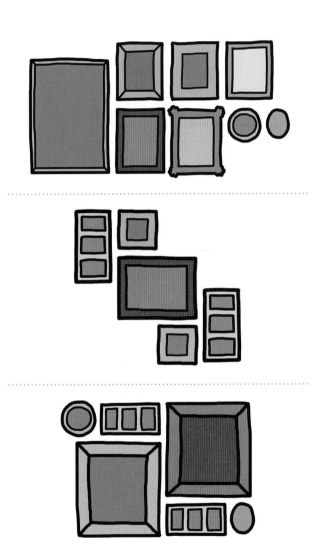

Art Height

The ideal height for art in any space depends more on the size of the art itself than the size of the wall: the center of the piece should be around 58 inches from the floor.

There are exceptions, of course: If there's a piece of furniture below, like a sofa or bed, the art should start around 6 to 8 inches above the top of the item. And if the walls in your house are super tall, the art can go a little higher to fill the space.

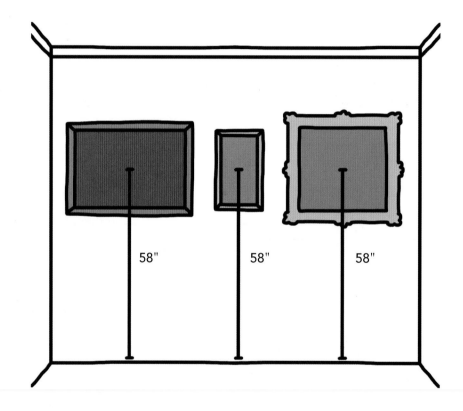

Types of Lighting

Choosing what style of light you want is a matter of taste, but the type of lighting option you need for a particular space is a matter of function. Lighting that is mounted to the ceiling, such as chandeliers, pendant lights, and flush mounts, provides ambient lighting for a large space. Sconces and other small, focused light sources provide decorative lighting. Table, floor, and task lights are geared toward a specific space and function, such as reading. Most rooms need a combination of multiple lighting sources in different areas.

Chandelier

Sconce

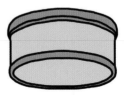

Flush Mount

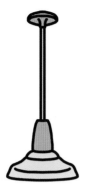

Pendant Light

Table Lamp

Floor Lamp

Task Light

Kinds of Lampshades

Use three important sizes to measure your lampshade: the top diameter, the bottom diameter, and the height. The style and size of your ideal lampshade will depend on the style and size of the lamp base, the wattage of the bulb, and where the lamp is going. The higher the wattage, the farther the bulb needs to be from the shade. Most new shades include maximum wattage recommendations.

MODERN

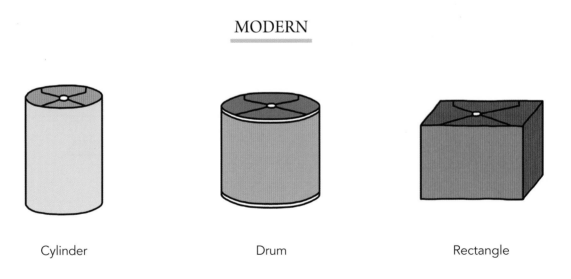

| Cylinder | Drum | Rectangle |

TRANSITIONAL

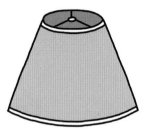

Empire

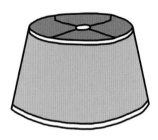

Tapered Drum

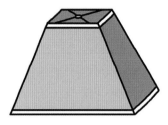

Tapered Square

CLASSIC

Bell

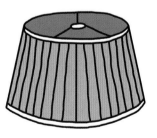

English Pleat

Pagoda

Scalloped

Table Lamp Styles

The ideal height for table lampshades is two-thirds the height of the base. For lamps with a solid, thick base, the width of the lampshade should be around twice the width of the base. Lamps that will sit on small or low tables or nightstands should have narrower shades to avoid being bumped. The simpler a lamp's base design is, the more types of shades will work on it. Round or wide lamps often look better with more classic shade styles and squared or thin lamps look better with modern or square shades.

Candlestick

Desk

Mid-Century

Modern

Tiffany

Urn

Floor Lamp Styles

There isn't an ideal size for floor lampshade size, but a good rule of thumb is that the switch should not be visible. Near a seating area, the bottom of the shade should be at least 1 foot higher than the top of the nearest piece of furniture.

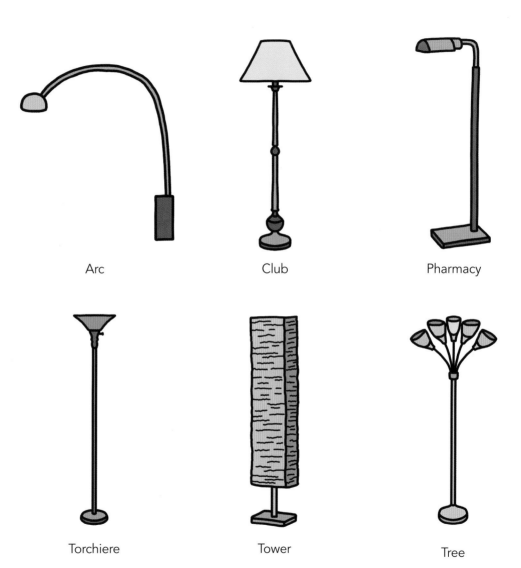

Arc

Club

Pharmacy

Torchiere

Tower

Tree

Hanging Light Height

Pendant or chandeliers above furniture should be low enough to cast light on the surface below them. They can be hung lower than other lights since no one will be walking beneath them. For dining room lighting, the bottom of the fixture should be 30 to 34 inches above the table. Above a kitchen island, the bottom of the light should be 30 inches above the highest part of the countertop. Lighting that is hung above a coffee table can be fairly low, 5 to 7 feet above the ground, as long as the fixture is smaller than the area of the table it's above. For larger fixtures, it should be high enough that the tallest person in your household clears the light.

TABLE

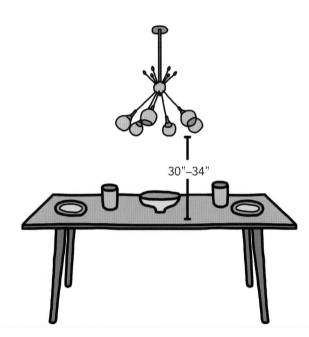

30"–34"

KITCHEN ISLAND

30"

LIVING ROOM

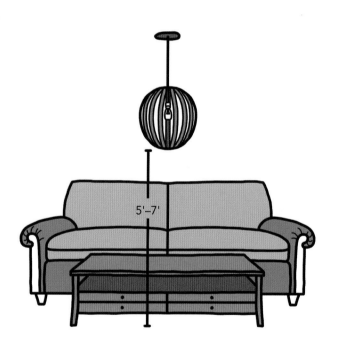

5'–7'

Places You Need Light

Aside from the obvious areas, lots of little spaces in your home that you might not think about could use extra lighting. To figure out where you need extra lighting, turn on all the lights in your home and look for places that are still in shadow or complete darkness, like closets, underneath cabinets, and along the stairs. Standing or decorative mirrors are often poorly lit, and extra lighting beside them will not only make them more functional, but will also bounce off the mirror's expanding light into the rest of the room.

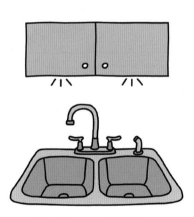

Under Cabinets

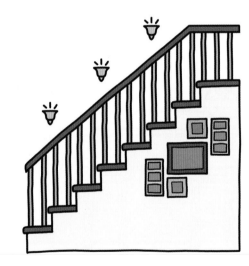

Along the Stairs

Next to the Front Door

In the Closet

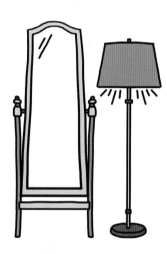

Beside the Mirror

Bathroom Light Tricks

Light in a bathroom is a big deal, especially if it's also the place you get ready every day. The worst kind is the generic pendant or flush mount in the bathroom ceiling, which causes unflattering shadows and distortion. A better solution is a bar light or multiple lights above the mirror, which will cast light on all sides and offset some of the shadows. The trick for the best, most flattering light is to put sconces on either side of the mirror, positioning the bottom of the shade or sconce at your eye level, or around 65 inches from the floor.

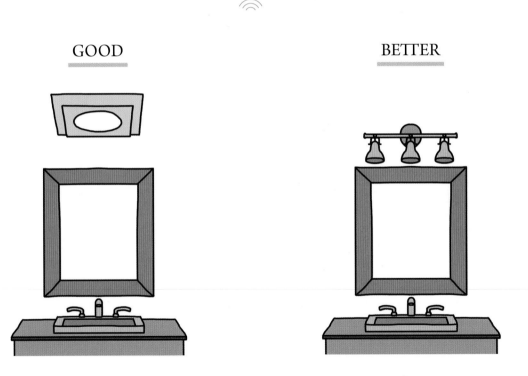

GOOD

BETTER

BEST

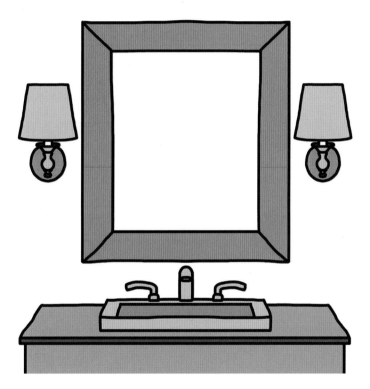

Parts of a Lamp

If your lamp feels too short, one cost-effective solution is to get a taller harp, which can usually be found at a hardware or lamp store. While the ideal lampshade is two-thirds the size of the lamp base, a few inches of height can sometimes make a big difference in the amount of light a lamp provides to certain areas of your home. Just make sure the harp is still small enough to be completely hidden by the shade.

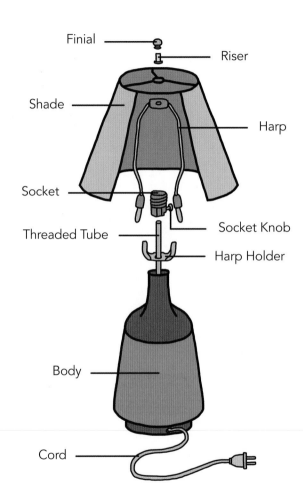

Finial — Riser

Shade

Harp

Socket

Socket Knob

Threaded Tube

Harp Holder

Body

Cord

HARDWARE
& CABINETRY

Cabinet Knobs

Cabinet knobs are much more about style and preference than function. While most cabinets are predrilled for a certain type of knob, replacing the original option is a cost-effective way to give cabinets a new look. Round knobs and arch pulls are more classic and traditional while square knobs and bar pulls have a more modern feel. For simplicity, many designers prefer to match cabinet hardware to the sink fixtures.

Round Knob

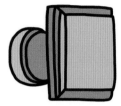

Square Knob

Arch Pull

Bar Pull

Cup Pull

Drop Pull

Edge Pull

Ring Pull

Loop Pull

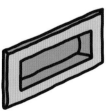

Recessed Pull

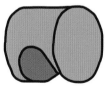

Finger Pull

Doorknobs

The two major types of door handles, grip-and-turn knobs and lever handles, both have pros and cons. Other than aesthetic preference, you should choose your handle based on the needs of your household.

TYPES OF HANDLES

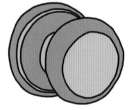

LEVER

Ergonomic for people with limited mobility. Easier for kids and animals to open. Can catch on clothing/elbows/straps. Must be matched to the door swing (whether the door opens on the left side or right side).

GRIP-AND-THEN-TURN KNOB

Harder for kids and animals to open. Can work with any door swing (left hand vs. right hand). Harder for people with limited mobility (or full/wet hands) to open.

TYPES OF LOCKS

PASSAGE

This type of knob is used on any interior doors in a home that do not need to be locked, but should open from both sides, such as a walk-in closet or hallway door.

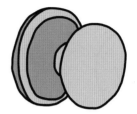

DUMMY

This is a single-sided knob that is used for any door that doesn't need to have a latched closure or open from both sides, such as a shallow closet.

PRIVACY

These types of knobs are used anywhere someone would need privacy (not security), such as a bathroom and bedroom.

KEYED

These are used in any interior areas that need to be securely locked, such as a back door.

Lightbulbs

TYPES OF BULBS

Incandescent

CFL

LED

BULB STYLES

Arbitrary

Globe

Spot

Bulged

Candle

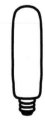

Tubular

Beginner's Guide to Lumens

Lumens is a unit of measure for the amount of light a bulb puts out. The number of lumens needed for a room or area depends on the size of the space, the activities that are performed there, and other factors, like wall paint or covering, which can absorb or reflect light depending on the finish and color. Watts, on the other hand, is actually the unit of measure for how much electricity a lightbulb requires to be illuminated. That's why a certain light fixture will require a maximum wattage of bulb. Different types of bulbs with the same wattage can actually produce the same amount of lumens, or visible light.

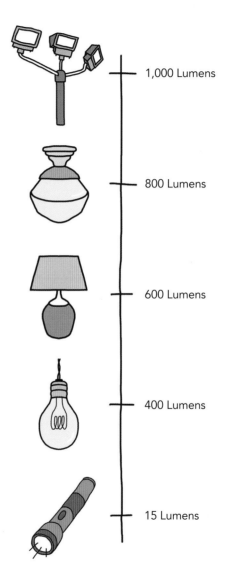

1,000 Lumens

800 Lumens

600 Lumens

400 Lumens

15 Lumens

Screws

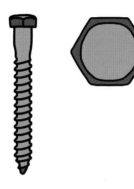

CAP SCREW

Used with bolts and has no screw head. Can be used for an extra-tight hold.

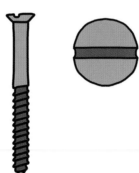

LAG SCREW

Usually large and with a hex head, these are used for heavy-duty materials.

MACHINE SCREW

Meant to be used with bolts, having no sharp point.

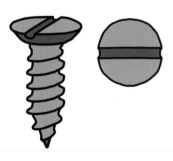

SELF-TAPPING SCREW

The point on these is designed to drill itself through the material. Can be found in wood, metal, and other varieties.

WOOD SCREW

These have a tapered shank and are used in securing wood.

Screw Heads

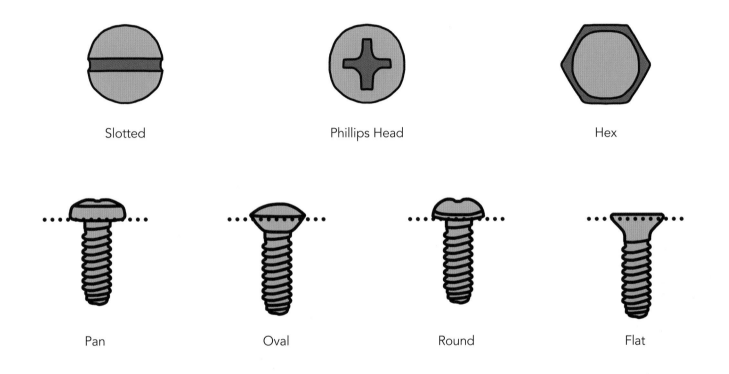

Slotted

Phillips Head

Hex

Pan

Oval

Round

Flat

Nails

COMMON NAIL

Can be purchased in many lengths. This is the most common type of nail used in rough construction, usually in wood.

BOX NAIL

These are smaller than common nails, but they are also not as strong.

FINISHING NAIL

These are used when the nail itself will show in the finished product, like on molding, because the head is small.

CASING NAIL

This is similar to a finishing nail, but stronger.

BRAD

A tiny version of the finishing nail that's used in small projects, like framing.

ROOFING NAIL

The large head of these nails is used to hold roofing material on tightly.

DRYWALL NAIL

These nails have rings around the shaft, designed to hold drywall together.

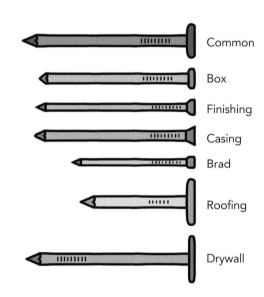

DESIGN & DECOR TRICKS

How to Make A Floor Plan

If you're getting any professional or contract work done, you'll want to have a professional floor plan made of your home. But for the DIY decorator and furniture shopper, a basic hand-drawn floor plan can be a big help in choosing what to buy and laying out your space.

While it's nice to draw a floor plan to scale, it's not necessary for this kind of layout. As long as you have accurate measurements for each space and element, it will still work. Ideally, you should note each measurement to the nearest ⅛ inch. Don't forget to measure on either side of each door, and account for how wide the door swings open.

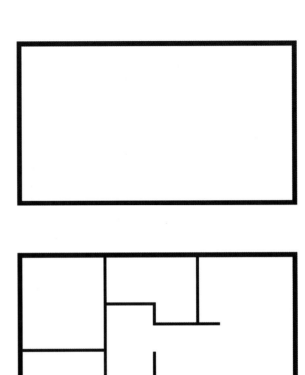

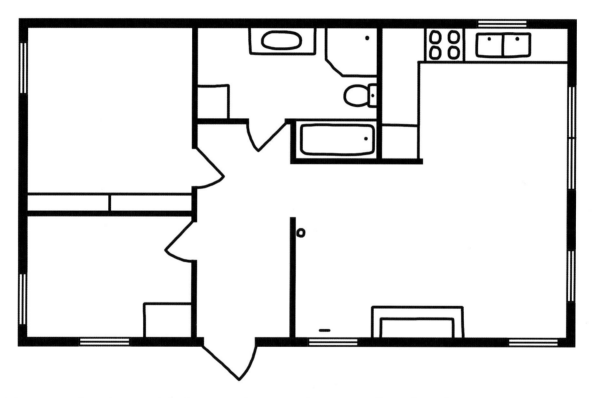

PRO TIP: Making note of windows and the location of power outlets on your floor plan will help you determine where to put lighting or large electronics so you don't have cords running too far.

Flow of a House

The flow of a house is essentially the way people walk or move through a space: walking through a hallway to get to a bedroom, moving through the living room to reach the kitchen, walking through a bedroom to the ensuite bathroom, etc. Knowing how your home flows will help you decide where to place certain pieces of furniture and where to put the focal point of each room (more on that next). A good rule of thumb for planning the space flow is this: think of how you would walk through the house with the lights off—anything that you could run into or trip over should be moved.

Flow can also be enhanced by using one color or color palette throughout the natural path of the house. Whether it's accessories in one color or artwork or accent paint in another color, a cohesive accent palette along the flow lines can really tie a space together.

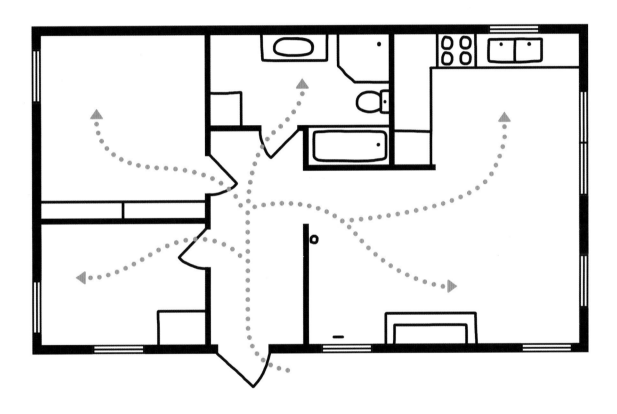

Focal Points

Each room or area of a house should have a visual "focal point." Some rooms have a natural focal point, like a fireplace or picture window. Others have chosen focal points, like a TV or gallery wall. If you're not sure where it is in a room, think of where your eye naturally goes when you enter the space, and work from there.

Large spaces or rooms in an open floor plan often have multiple focal points, like a large window in one space and a big sofa or large piece of art in another. This can serve to break up a room and visually divide the space into specific areas.

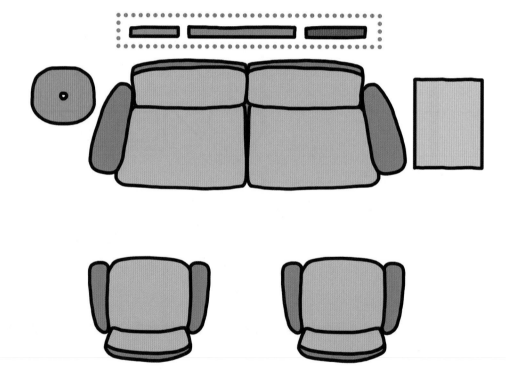

Layers of Light

Having at least three "layers" of light in any area will give the space depth and allow you to adjust the atmosphere to reflect what's happening there. Each layer consists of a different light source or group of light sources that serve a similar function. The three basic layers of light are: ambient, accent, and task lighting. These three layers can be used together to achieve maximum illumination (like at nighttime when tasks are being performed) or used separately to set the mood or direct attention to a particular area.

Ambient lighting is the most basic layer. Sometimes called overhead lighting, ambient light illuminates the entire room and is usually bright and somewhat harsh. The most common source is recessed or flush-mount, chandeliers, or ceiling fans with lights attached. People often stop at this layer without considering the other functions of the room.

Accent, or decorative, lighting is used to highlight particular objects or elements in a space. This can be specific, like a directional light above a painting, or more broad, like track lighting above a certain wall. This is also used in outdoor lighting design, like directional floodlights pointing to certain trees or architectural features.

Task lighting is any specific fixture aimed at helping you accomplish a particular task: It includes things like desk lamps, reading lamps, and table and floor lamps. The need and location of this kind of light will change more frequently than the other two layers, as the use of each space or arrangement of furniture changes.

Certain fixtures can be used for multiple layers of light; for instance, a chandelier or overhead light with a dimming switch would serve as ambient light at the highest level and accent light when lowered.

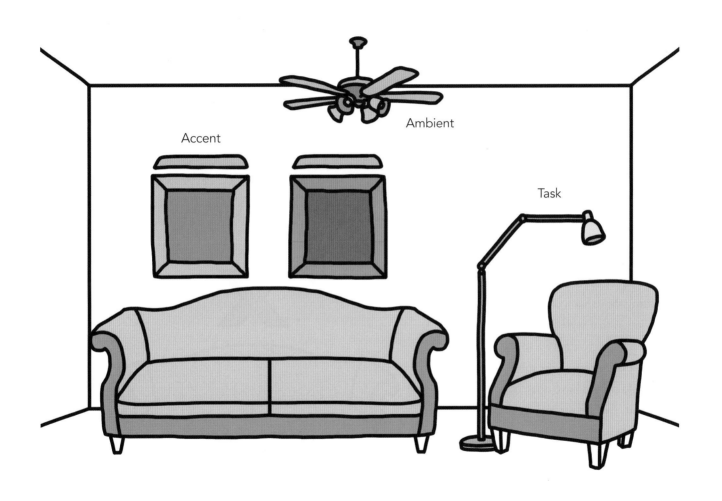

Accent

Ambient

Task

Proportion and Scale

Proportion and scale refer to the size of each furnishing in relation to the other. All rooms need large, medium, and small items, and the style and location of each contributes to the balance and completeness of the space.

Proportion and scale are also a factor in the function of the space: if you have an extra-long sofa, you need a similarly proportioned coffee table so that everyone sitting there has a place to put a drink. The key is that style and size contribute to scale: if you have a sofa with a skirt so the bottom looks solid, your coffee table should have open legs to balance it out. But if your sofa has legs with space visible below, your table can be a little heavier. It's all about balance.

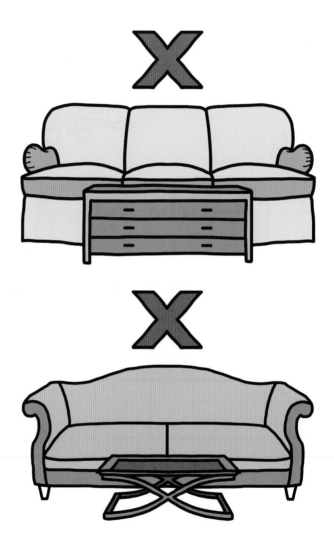

Curtain Height

You might not be able to raise your ceilings or widen your windows, but you can use your curtains to trick the eye into thinking you have. Basic curtain height and width covers only the exact size of the window. A better way to make the window seem even wider is to get a curtain rod that's about 1 foot longer than the actual window, so that when the shades are open, they don't cover any of the actual window. This allows for maximum light to come in and also makes the window look like it's even bigger. The best way to use curtains is to hang them closer to the ceiling than to the top of the window, as well as wider than the frame. This draws the eye upward, makes the ceilings seem taller, and allows for maximum light when the curtains are open.

GOOD

BETTER

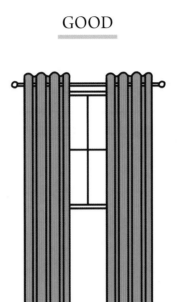

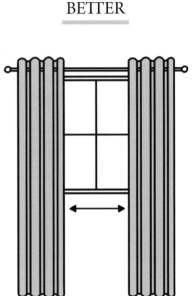

BEST

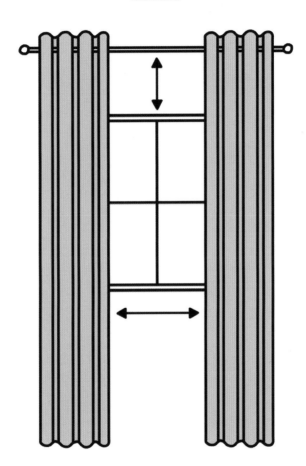

Best Indoor Plants

Plants are a wonderful way to add warmth and color to any space. The best kind of plant to get depends on the orientation and size of the room's windows and where the plant will go. South-facing windows provide the most light and north-facing windows provide the least. East and west-facing windows both provide medium light that's short-lived, especially in winter months, so plants should be placed closer to the windows for optimum health. If you want to keep plants in a room with low/no light, move them into a room with light every two weeks.

LOW LIGHT

Chinese Evergreen

Peace Lily

Pothos

Snake Plant

Spider Plant

MEDIUM LIGHT

Fiddle Leaf Fig

Prayer Plant

Boston Fern

Bird's Nest Fern

Rubber Plant

Furniture Redo

If you don't want to invest in new furniture, but are tired of a particular style, there are several ways to update old pieces to make them look fresh and new. The two cheapest and easiest ways to redo furniture are to swap out the hardware or the legs. Cabinets and other drawers can be transformed with a new style of knob. Sofa and chair legs can often be easily swapped for more modern or sleek designs. Painting and reupholstering are more time-consuming and costly, but are a great way to give old or thrifted furniture new life. Basic painting and upholstery projects can be DIYed, and even a custom upholstery job can be less expensive than a new piece.

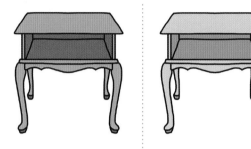

Painting

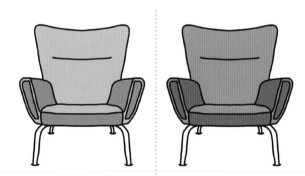

Reupholstering

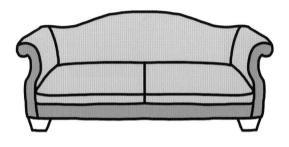

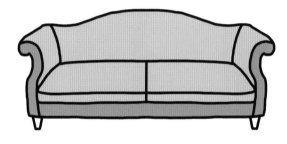

Swapping Hardware

Changing Legs

Fabric Yardage: Chairs

Vintage French

2 yards

Tub

4 yards

Modern Wingback

7 yards

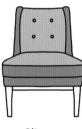

Bergère

5 yards

Slipper

5 yards

Parsons

3 yards

Wingback

7 yards

Lawson

6 yards

Club

8 yards

Occasional

3 yards

Fabric Yardage: Sofas

Cabriole

6 feet: 12 yards
7 feet: 14 yards
9 feet: 18 yards

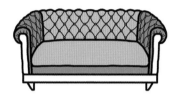

Chesterfield

6 feet: 13 yards
7 feet: 15 yards
9 feet: 20 yards

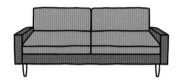

Mid-Century

6 feet: 13 yards
7 feet: 15 yards
9 feet: 20 yards

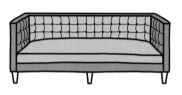

Tuxedo

6 feet: 13 yards
7 feet: 15 yards
9 feet: 20 yards

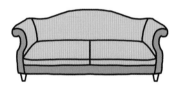

Camelback

6 feet: 12 yards
7 feet: 14 yards
9 feet: 18 yards

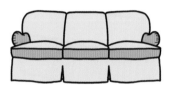

English Roll Arm

6 feet: 13 yards
7 feet: 15 yards
9 feet: 20 yards

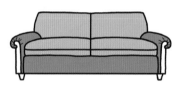

Lawson

6 feet: 12 yards
7 feet: 15 yards
9 feet: 18 yards

Settee

7 yards

Daybed

5 yards

Chaise

8 yards

Fabric Yardage: Beds

UPHOLSTERED HEADBOARD

King: 3 yards

Queen: 2.5 yards

Full: 2 yards

Twin: 2 yards

Resource Guide

Apartment Therapy
apartmenttherapy.com

Apartment Therapy is the go-to blog for small-space solutions and inspiring tours of smaller homes with great, achievable style.

BuzzFeed DIY
buzzfeed.com/diy

BuzzFeed DIY is a great resource for easy-to-use tips on renovations, decor, organization, smart-living tips, and products for the home.

Decor8
decor8blog.com

Decor8 was one of the first design blogs to take off, launched by Holly Becker in 2006. The blog covers all manner of home-related tips, from DIYs to styling tips to recipes.

Design Sponge
designsponge.com

Design Sponge is a great place for inspiration on how to live and work creatively.

Domino
domino.com

Domino is a one-stop design destination for fresh and fashionable interior design inspiration with shoppable photo galleries and their own line of home products.

Remodelaholic
remodelaholic.com

Remodelaholic is a DIY blog about remodeling on a budget, with great resources and tips on how to make hard projects easier.

The Sill
thesill.com

The Sill is a shop for indoor plants that also happens to be a great resource on how to keep your existing plants alive.

Style by Emily Henderson
stylebyemilyhenderson.com

Emily Henderson is a designer and stylist who is great at making complicated design topics super easy to understand and apply in your own home.

The Sweet Home
thesweethome.com

The Sweet Home does thorough and spot-on review of anything you'd need in your home, from furnishings and appliances to tools and techniques.

Vintage Revivals
vintagerevivals.com

Vintage Revivals is a DIY and design blog with great tips on how to make thrifted furniture look better than new.

Acknowledgments

Thanks to all my bosses, mentors, and teachers, and my parents, who always valued creativity as much as any other skill or subject. Thanks to all the people who hired me throughout the years, despite my having the most random string of jobs and experiences. Thanks to the founders and my fellow designers at Homepolish for creating such inspirational and accessible spaces. And thanks to all my hilarious, intelligent, hard-working, and creative colleagues at BuzzFeed, especially the genius illustrator Alice, who can take a string of words and a terrible sketch and turn it into something delightful.

—*Jessica Probus*

I want to thank my mom for her never-ending love and support. Thank you, Michael, for literally being by my side night after night, assuring me that the chair I was drawing actually looked like a chair. Thank you, Loki, for always being just an arm's reach away for all those times I needed a break. Thank you to all my friends who cheered me on. And, of course, thank you Jessica for giving me this amazing opportunity to make the book come to life.

—*Alice Mongkongllite*

About the Contributors

Jessica Probus is a writer, editor, and designer living and working in New York City. She has worked as an interior designer, set designer, prop stylist, and production designer in New York and Atlanta. She is currently the DIY editor at BuzzFeed and a designer at HomePolish, and she lives in Queens with her partner and an ever-growing collection of plants.

Alice Mongkongllite is a graphic designer and illustrator based in Los Angeles. She graduated from UCLA with a degree in design/media arts and has since worked at an advertising agency, mobile gaming startup, and in various cafés around the world while freelancing. She is currently a graphic designer at BuzzFeed. Her obsessions include DIY culture, pretty stationery, and her dog Loki. She lives in Los Angeles with her husband.